BADMINTON
ENGLAND
Play it. Love it. Live it.

Badminton

Produced in collaboration
with BADMINTON England

Produced for Bloomsbury by

Monkey Puzzle Media Ltd
Little Manor Farm, The Street, Brundish
Woodbridge, Suffolk IP13 8BL

Published in 2006 by

Bloomsbury Publishing PLC
50 Bedford Square, London WC1B 3DP
www.acblack.com

Reprinted 2008, 2011
Fourth edition 2006

Note: While every effort has been made to ensure
that the content of this book is as technically accurate
and as sound as possible, neither the author nor the
publisher can accept responsibility for any injury or
loss sustained as a result of the use of this material.

Bloomsbury uses paper produced with elemental
chlorine-free pulp, harvested from managed
sustainable forests.

Acknowledgements
Thanks to the following at BADMINTON England:
George Wood, Jonathan Ponsford and Mike
Woodward. Thanks also to Paul Trueman (Badminton
coach) and Jill Brill (National Badminton Museum).
Cover and inside design by James Winrow for
Monkey Puzzle Media Ltd.
Front cover photograph courtesy of Getty Images. All
other photographs courtesy of BADMINTON England
and Alan Spink (Action Photography).
Illustrations by Margaret Jones.

KNOW THE GAME is a registered trademark.

Printed and bound in China by C&C Offset Printing

Note: Throughout the book players and officials are
referred to as 'he'. This should, of course, be taken to
mean 'he or she' where appropriate. Similarly, all
instructions are geared towards right-handed players
– left-handers should simply reverse these instructions.

CONTENTS

A SHORT HISTORY

Around 1860, the daughters of the Duke of Beaufort were playing a popular children's game called 'battledore and shuttle-cock'. The battledore was a paddle, which they used to keep the shuttlecock in the air as long as possible. Their 'court' was the great hall of Badminton House, a stately home in Gloucestershire, England. To add a little variety, they rigged up a string across the hall, from the doorway to the fireplace: the aim of the new game was to try to keep the shuttle going by playing it to each other over the string. It is said that a Mr J. L. Baldwin suggested it would be more fun if the shuttle were hit away from, instead of towards, players on the other side of the string. The sport of badminton had been created.

By the mid- to late 1870s, indoor badminton clubs were being formed in England. Soon, clubs were pitting their skills against each other in competition. There were no shuttlecock manufacturers at that time, so players had to make their own from whatever materials were available. There were no laws governing the size of the court, its markings, player numbers or scoring until 1893, when the forerunner of BADMINTON England was formed.

Since that time, badminton has boomed in popularity. The International Badminton Federation (IBF) was formed in 1934 and organised its first major championship – the Thomas Cup – in 1948. The sport reached the Olympics as a demonstration sport in 1972 and achieved full-medal status at the 1992 Barcelona Olympics.

INDOOR GAME

Because of the extreme lightness of the shuttle, which is affected by the slightest breeze, badminton is mostly played indoors.

Fast and fit

Badminton is now generally rated, in its higher grades, as one of the fastest and most exhausting sports around. Good racket work, which can move the shuttle at ferocious speed, and the fact that the shuttle must not hit the floor are the main reasons for this.

▼ Badminton is a game of technical and tactical skill which at international level demands high levels of fitness.

A sport for all

Badminton can be played by men or women, young or old, and it is also thriving in sporting competitions for the disabled. Size or strength give no particular advantage. Badminton is also one of the few sports in which a woman can compete on equal terms in a partnership with a man. In fact, mixed doubles is regarded as one of the most entertaining forms of badminton.

THE GAME

Badminton can be played recreationally at little or no expense – whether it is a fun 'hit' in the garden or a more competitive game in a sports centre. Badminton is played competitively at many levels, from local league club matches and beginner tournaments to the World Championships and the Olympic Games.

Badminton is played on a court by two players (singles) or four players (doubles). The players use rackets to hit a shuttle over a net from one side to the other. The object of the game is to hit the shuttle across the net:

- to a place on the opponent's court where it cannot be reached
- to force the opponent to hit the shuttle out of the court
- to force the opponent to hit it into the net.

Under the traditional scoring system, achieving this earns your side a point when you or your partner has served.

The first player or pair to reach the required number of points in a game wins that game. A badminton match is played over the best of three games.

THE COURT

The surface of the court should be of wood, although other surfaces can be used if they are not slippery.

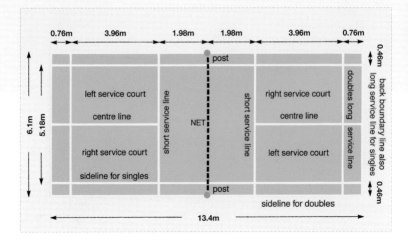

The shuttle is usually white, so the floor and background should be of a dark shade to make the shuttle visible. If painted, the floor and background should not be glossy, as reflection makes sighting the shuttle difficult.

The court markings must be clearly defined, preferably with white lines. Yellow lines may be used if this helps distinguish the court markings from markings on the floor used for other sports. In either case, the lines should be 40mm wide. All lines form part of the area that they define: the edge of the court, for example, is the outside edge of the line.

THE NET AND POSTS

The net is suspended from net posts, which must be placed on the outer sidelines. They must not intrude onto the court. There should be no gaps between the ends of the net and the posts.

The posts themselves should not be higher than 1.55m. This is important, as, by their position on the sidelines, they actually stand within the playing area. Posts come in a variety of types. Some come with fittings that screw into the floor. Others stand upright and stable via a weighted base.

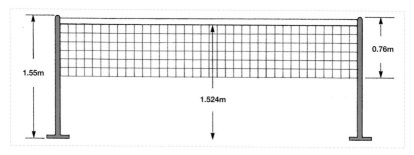

1.55m 0.76m 1.524m

The badminton net and posts.

The badminton court and its dimensions.

COURT JARGON

Players and coaches often break the court into three areas:

- forecourt – the front third of the court
- midcourt – the middle third of the court
- rearcourt – the back third of the court.

Service areas

Each side of a court features a left and right service area. These service areas are where players must stand both to serve and to receive the serve. The receiver must stand in the area until after the serve has been delivered:

- a foot on or touching a line in the case of either the server or the receiver is held to be outside the service court and therefore is a fault

- the centre line dividing the right and left service areas is regarded as 'in court' for either side should the shuttle fall on that line.

A SUITABLE HALL

The height of the hall over the whole area of the court should be:

- 7.6m for a Development Centre
- 9.1m for a Performance and Development Centre.

A hall with a slightly lower roof can be used, but it would not be suitable for first-class play.

There should be at least 2.5m between the wall and the baseline and at least 2.3m between any wall and the sidelines of the court. The background should be uniform in colour with the walls finished in medium to dark shades with a matt surface.

 An approved badminton hall with the important measurements and dimensions.

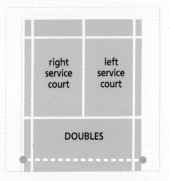

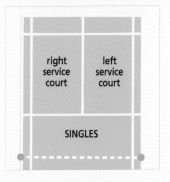

 Parallel sidelines are commonly known as 'tramlines'.

When the court is permanently in use for badminton the best posts to use are those with a metal base that can be screwed to the floor.

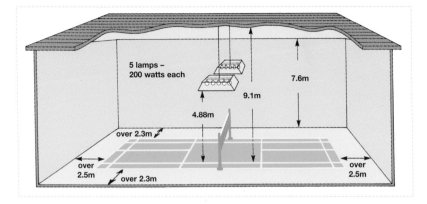

```
5 lamps –
200 watts each

7.6m

9.1m

4.88m

over 2.3m

over
2.5m        over 2.3m

over
2.5m
```

Daylight

Daylight, if any, should come from above, through skylights on the north or east side of the building. This helps avoid sun glare which can be very troubling to players. If windows are necessary for other reasons, then they must have curtains or blinds that can be drawn across when badminton is being played.

View of a typical badminton court.

Artificial lighting

Good light can be provided by two groups of lamps positioned on each side of the court. These lamps should be:

- 4.88m from the floor
- 0.6 to 0.9m outside, and parallel to, the sidelines
- centralised over the net.

Each fitting should, ideally, have a line of tungsten opaque lamps totalling at least 1,000 watts. These may be either hung directly from the roof or fixed to posts.

> **FURTHER INFORMATION**
>
> A pamphlet with details of halls suitable for badminton is available from BADMINTON England (see page 53 for contact details).

EQUIPMENT

Rapid technical advances mean that the rackets used by the top players 20 years ago have been surpassed by the lightweight models readily available today to all players. By contrast, the design and construction of the shuttlecock hasn't noticeably changed in recent years. For a beginner, badminton is a relatively low cost sport to start playing.

THE RACKET

Modern badminton rackets can weigh less than 100g, which enables them to be moved with tremendous speed. They can vary between a one-piece graphite construction and those with titanium mesh inserts on the head. There are also differences in head size and shape – variations intended to increase the 'sweet spot' of the racket (the area of the racket's strings that offers the best combination of feel and power).

Test as many rackets within your price range as possible, before deciding which to buy.

THE SHUTTLE

There are two basic types of shuttle: feathered or synthetic. The feathered shuttle is very fragile, weighs only 4–6g and is more expensive than the synthetic type. It is made from 16 goose feathers inserted in a cork base and is generally used for any serious competitive play.

 The official dimensions of a shuttlecock.

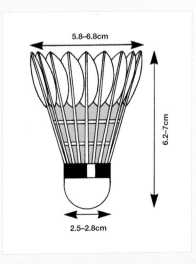

5.8–6.8cm

6.2–7cm

2.5–2.8cm

Synthetic shuttles feature a skirt of synthetic material replacing the natural feathers. The base may also be synthetic. They are more durable, inexpensive and widely used by beginners and club players.

Shuttle speeds

A shuttle's speed and flight varies depending on the atmosphere in a hall as well as its size and temperature. As a result, shuttles are made that play at different speeds.

Law 4 of the Laws of Badminton says: 'A shuttle shall be deemed to be of correct pace when it is hit by a player with a full underhand stroke from a spot immediately above one back boundary line in a direction parallel to the sidelines and at an upward angle, to fall not less than 530mm and not more than 990mm short of the other back boundary line.'

Feathered shuttles should be treated with great care and never hit along the floor. Once the feathers become damaged, the flight will be affected.

Recent tests have shown that the shuttle can leave a modern racket at an incredible speed of over 200 miles per hour (320km/h).

DRESS

Because badminton is a fast game, freedom of movement is essential. Court clothing should be comfortable and stay comfortable throughout the game. Shorts and shirt are the usual clothing. Badminton is sometimes played in inadequately heated halls: a sweatshirt and/or tracksuit is useful for warmth when knocking-up and starting a game.

Footwear

Having the right shoes is important: uncomfortable shoes hamper performance. Shoes should be specialist badminton/indoor court shoes, and should not have black soles that could mark the court floor. They are usually worn with suitable sports socks to prevent blisters on your feet.

VERSIONS OF THE GAME

Although the singles and doubles disciplines are fundamentally similar, the differences in speed, tactics and type of fitness required are considerable, particularly at higher levels where the majority of top players specialise in either singles or doubles. The mixed doubles game makes badminton one of the few sports where women can compete on equal terms with men.

THE DOUBLES GAME

The doubles game is the most common in badminton played in England. Before the game starts the opponents 'toss'. This can be done using a coin, but is more commonly achieved by striking a shuttle in the air and leaving it to fall. The side deemed to have won the toss is the one that the base of the shuttle points to.

Winning the toss gives one side first choice of one of the following:

- to serve first
- not to serve first, or
- which side of the court to start play.

The side losing the toss has a choice of the remaining alternatives.

Starting the game

The pair delivering the opening service decides which player will serve. The receiving pair decides which player will receive the first service.

The first service must be delivered from the right-hand service court and directed to the diagonally opposite court, i.e. the receiver's right-hand court, as shown in the diagram.

In a match played over the best of three games, the side winning the previous game serves first in the next game.

> **The pair serving is referred to as the 'in' side, and the pair receiving the 'out' side.**

THE SINGLES GAME

A singles game also begins with a toss, with the winner choosing an end, deciding to serve or opting not to serve in the same way as with doubles.

Singles games use a different area of the court to doubles. The side tramlines are not used at all for singles, making the court 1m less wide. The service court in singles is extended to the baseline at the very back of the court. This makes the singles service area long and thin.

In singles, a player loses serve if they lose one rally on their serve. The laws provide for service to be delivered from both the left and right sides of the court. Servers in a singles game serve from the right-hand service court when their score is '0' or any even number. They serve from the left-hand service court when their score is an odd number.

In the first service in a doubles game, the server (**A**) stands in the right-hand court and delivers the serve to the diagonally opposite court (**X**).

Singles service: (**a**) serving from the left-hand service court to left-hand service court – score is odd; (**b**) serving from the right-hand service court to right-hand service court – score is 0 or even.

SERVICE

The serve is an extremely important part of badminton, especially in doubles. Under the traditional scoring system it is only the serving side that can add points to their score when they win a rally, so a good serve is essential. A number of rules exist to ensure that the server does not gain an unfair advantage when serving.

MAKING THE SERVICE

To make a correct service you must:

- wait until the receiver is ready
- stand within the limits of your own service court
- have some part of both feet stationary on the ground until the service has been delivered
- hit the shuttle directly over the net into the service court diagonally opposite
- ensure the service action is one continuous forward movement from start to finish. The server must not make any feint with the intention of deceiving their opponent before or during the service.

At the moment that the racket first hits the shuttle:

- the shuttle must be below the waist
- the whole racket head must be discernibly below the hand holding the racket
- the racket must make first contact with the shuttle's base, not its feathers.

If the server does not perform all eight of the above points, it is a service fault and they lose the service.

A common service fault is for the racket to hit the shuttle when the shuttle is above waist height.

Order of service – traditional scoring

In the doubles game, both players get a chance to serve. Only when both players have lost their serve does the service pass to the opposition. There is one exception: at the start of the game, the team serving first only gets one of their players to serve. When the player loses serve, it passes to the other side.

Each rally a serving side wins earns a point. After each winning rally, the server switches service courts. The opposition players stay in the service courts where they were at the start of the rally. This means that they receive alternate serves. Having just won the right to serve, the player in the right-hand court goes first and upon losing a rally the service passes to the partner. Should the side lose another rally, the service goes back once more to the opposition.

For example, during the middle of a game, player 1 serves from the right-hand court and wins a rally. Player 1's side gains a point and 1 serves again, this time from the left-hand service court. Player 1's side loses this rally. Next, 1's team mate (player 2) serves. Player 2 serves, wins the rally and serves again, switching service courts. On losing the rally, service passes over to the opposing team with the player in the right-hand service court starting. Both players get the chance to serve in the same way.

Singles is similar in that each player serves once, and the winner of the rally serves the next point.

Order of service – 'rally point' scoring

With rally point scoring each side gets one service, in both singles and doubles. If the serving side has an even score, they serve from the right-hand service court. Likewise, a player will serve from the left service court if their score is an odd number.

No player is allowed to cause undue delay at the service.

◀ This server has made a service fault by striking the shuttle while the head of the racket is above the hand.

RECEIVING THE SERVICE

As the receiver you should stand within the limits of the service court diagonally opposite the server. Your feet must be entirely within the lines marking the boundary of the court, and must not touch them. As with the server, one part of both feet must remain stationary on the ground until the service is delivered.

Your stance is crucial when receiving service. You should have both knees flexed with your foot on the non-racket side of your body forwards. Your racket should be positioned in front of your body at net height or slightly above. Try to stay alert and focused on your opponent's service action and the flight path of the shuttle. Remember, you may have to react to a wide service, a short service or a long, high service.

Common faults

Sometimes, players stand in an upright position and keep their racket leg straight. This makes it very difficult for them to move quickly to the service. In many cases, this will mean that the shuttle is taken late when it is below net height. The opportunity to attack is therefore lost.

Players who do adopt an attacking stance may fail to make the most of it, purely by hitting the shuttle and then letting their racket drop. Once their racket head is below net height, it becomes impossible to play an attacking downward shot.

Receiving position

The receiver's actual position within the service area depends on personal choice. It is a good idea to stand as near as possible to the short-service line to be able to 'kill' a short service, but still be able to get back to a deep high service. This is a judgement players make for themselves based on their experience.

As the shuttle is served, the receiver has to decide whether the service will land inside the service court. If the service will not, the player can allow the shuttle to hit the floor and win the point. But if the shuttle does fall within the court or on the surrounding lines, the serve is good and the server wins a point.

Movement after service

As soon as the service has been delivered, players may move to any position for subsequent shots. They are allowed to leave the sides or back of their half of the court. The only restriction is that a player may not cross into their opponent's half of the court.

Look to stand on the balls of your feet, with your knees bent. This enables you to react and move quickly in any direction.

Mixed doubles pair Nathan Robertson and Gail Emms of England are poised ready to receive service.

TRADITIONAL SCORING

In this method of scoring, only the serving side can add points to its score when winning a rally. If the opponents win that particular rally they do not score a point but cause the server to lose the right to serve. When both partners have lost the right to serve, the service passes to the other side. They now get their chance to win rallies and add points to their score.

TRADITIONAL SCORING IN ACTION

Scoring in a typical game is illustrated by the text and diagrams below and on the opposite page. Team **AB** are playing **XY**. **AB** win the toss and decide to serve. Player **A** delivers the service and **X** decides to receive.

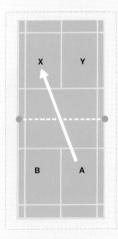

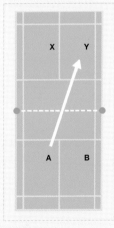

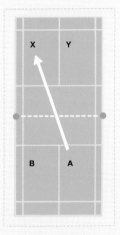

1. Player **A** serves from the right-hand court to **X** in **X**'s right-hand court. Team **AB** win the rally. The score is 1–0.

2. Player **A** now serves from the left-hand court to **Y** in **Y**'s left-hand court. Team **AB** win the rally. The score is 2–0.

3. Player **A** serves from the right-hand court to **X** in **X**'s right-hand court. Team **XY** win the rally.

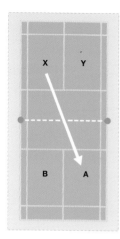 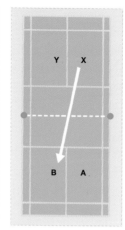 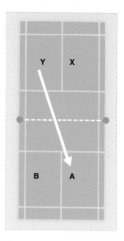

4. Service passes to **XY**. The score is 0–2 (the server's score is called first). Player **X**, being in the right-hand court, takes the service and serves to **A** who was in **A**'s right-hand court at the start of the last rally. Team **XY** win the rally. The score is 1–2.

5. Player **X** now serves from the opposite court to **B**. Team **AB** win the rally. **X** loses the right to serve and **Y** delivers the next service. The score is 1–2 (second server).

6. **Y** serves from the right-hand court, the court **Y** was in at the beginning of the last rally. Team **AB** win the rally. **Y** loses the service, and **Y**'s team loses the right to serve. Team **AB** take the service. The score is 2–1. **A** in the right-hand court will serve. **A** serves until **AB** lose a rally, then the service passes to **B**.

Points to win

In doubles and men's singles, a game is won by the first side to score 15 points. In ladies' singles, it is the first to 11 points. If the scores are 14-all (10-all in ladies' singles), the side which first scored 14 (10) can decide:

- to continue the game to 15 (11) points, or
- to 'set' the game to 17 (13) points (see page 24).

Changing ends

A match is normally the best of three games. Players should change ends:

- at the completion of the first game
- before the beginning of the third game, and
- in the third game when the leading score reaches 6 in a game of 11 points, or 8 in a game of 15 points.

RALLY POINT SCORING

The International Badminton Federation (IBF) has introduced an experimental scoring system of three games to 21 points with 'rally point' scoring. This means that a point is awarded to the winner of each rally regardless of who served. The system applies only to IBF-sanctioned events for the trial period. It is likely that the traditional method of scoring will be used at most levels of play for the immediate future.

RALLY POINT SCORING IN ACTION

Scoring in a typical 'rally point' game is illustrated by the diagrams below and on the opposite page. Team **AB** are playing **XY**. **AB** wins the toss and decide to serve. Player **A** delivers the service and **X** decides to receive.

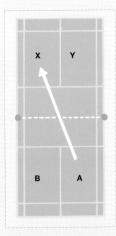 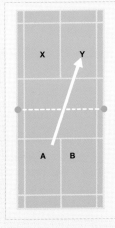 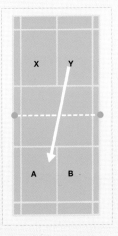

1. Player **A** serves from the right-hand court to **X** in **XY**'s right hand court. Team **AB** win the rally. The score is 1–0.

2. Player **A** now serves from the left-hand court to **Y** in **XY**'s left hand court. Team **XY** win the rally. The score is 1–1.

3. Player **Y** serves from the left hand court to **A** in **AB**'s left-hand court, as the score of the serving side is an odd number. Team **AB** win the rally. The score is 2–1 to team **AB**.

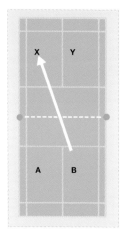 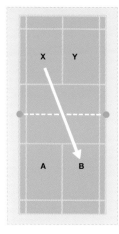 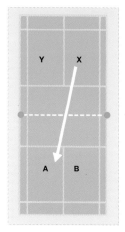

4. Service passes to player **B** who serves from the right-hand court to **X** in **XY**'s right-hand court, as the score of the serving side is even. Team **XY** win the rally. The score is 2–2.

5. Player **X** now serves back to **B**, due to the serving side still having an even score. Team **XY** win the rally, and they now lead 3–2.

6. Players **X** and **Y** change service courts, so that **X** now serves to **A** from the left-hand court. Should team **AB** win the rally, player **A** would serve from the left-hand court and nobody changes position, while a win for team **XY** would mean that they swap sides once more, with **X** serving again.

Points to win

In singles and doubles a game is won by the side that is first to score 21 points. This applies unless the score reaches 20–20, in which case:

- the side which gains a two point lead wins, or
- if the score reaches 29–29 the side that scores the 30th point will win the game.

Changing ends

A match is normally the best of three games. Players should change ends:

- at the completion of the first game
- before the beginning of the third game, and
- in the third game when the leading side scores 11 points.

FAULTS IN PLAY

In the majority of cases badminton matches are played without an umpire, which means that the players are required to have a sound knowledge of the laws and when they are applied. Occasionally slight changes have been made to the laws, such as the removal of faults for 'frame shots' – strokes where the shuttle strikes the frame of the racket.

A player's side loses the rally if:

- the player fails to return the shuttle over the net into the opponent's court

- when the shuttle is in play, the player touches the net or its supports with racket, person or clothing

- the player strikes the shuttle before it crosses to their side of the net

- the player touches the shuttle with any part of their body or clothing

- the player obstructs an opponent by, for example, sliding under the net or throwing a racket into an opponent's court

- the shuttle is caught and held on the racket and then slung

- the shuttle is hit twice in succession by the same player with two strokes

- the shuttle is hit by a player and the player's partner successively

- the server, in attempting to serve, misses the shuttle completely.

It is not a fault:

- to hit the base and feathers of the shuttle at the same time

- to strike the shuttle using any part of the racket frame or stem providing it is with one distinct hit

- in a rally, to play the shuttle round the outside of the net post as long as it falls within the opponent's court.

In the natural follow-through of a shot, your racket is allowed over the net providing it does not touch it.

LETS IN PLAY

The only occasion when a rally may be held up without one side or the other winning it, is when a 'let' is granted. A let may be claimed when there is an accidental interference during play, such as a shuttle from an adjacent court, or if the shuttle in play somehow gets caught in the net after passing over it.

A let can be claimed by the receiver if the server serves from the wrong service court and wins the rally. Similarly, a let can be claimed by the server, should the receivers have changed courts wrongly and won the rally.

You can only claim either of these last two lets straight after the rally has ended. If the error is only discovered later on, no let can be claimed and players continue to play from the courts they are in.

SERVICE LETS

Players sometimes call a service let if the shuttle touches the top of the net. In fact this rule was abolished from the game in 1958. If a shuttle in service touches the top of the net, play continues. Only if it does not fall into the service area it is a fault.

Jonas Rasmussen of Denmark returns the opponents' serve, taking the shuttle early.

SETTING

Setting – traditional scoring

When the score is level near the end of a game, each side appears to only need one further point to win. However, the first side that reaches that score has the option of playing to the next point (15 points or 11 in a ladies' singles game) to win the game, or of 'setting' the game.

When a game is set, it is won by the first side to reach 17 points (or 13 points in the ladies' singles game). For example, in the case of AB v XY, AB may be leading by 14 points to 11 in a 15-point game. XY regain the service and from their service win the next 3 points, bringing the score to 14 points all. Both sides now require 1 point to win the game. AB, being the first side to reach 14 points, now has the option of setting the game. AB opt to set and the first side to reach 17 points wins the game.

Setting – rally point scoring

Players do not have the option of setting under the rally point scoring method. Instead, if the score reaches 20–20, the side which next takes a two-point lead will win the game. If neither side has opened up a two-point margin by the time the score reaches 29–29, the winners will be the team to win the next rally.

Choosing to set

In the majority of cases, a player or pair will choose to set rather than not. This is primarily because declining the option immediately puts that side within one point of losing the match, as the opponent has the serve. In doubles matches, a side may decide not to set if the opposing pair only has one serve remaining, and if they win the next rally they would then have two serves to win the game.

Chen Jin of China demonstrates great athleticism as he prepares to hit an overhead forehand shot.

THE STROKES

Players use height, depth and width of the court to put their opponents under pressure. It is therefore essential that players have the ability to play a variety of shots in order to successfully compete and play the most appropriate return. Playing the right stroke with the right grip is a vital aspect in taking the first step to improving your game.

GRIP

Grips should be relaxed, with a tightening on impact. The degree of tightening depends on how hard you want to hit the shuttle – the more you tighten as the racket goes to the shuttle the harder you will hit it.

Basic

The basic grip is a fingers and palm grip, with a 'V' being created between the thumb and first finger. The point of the 'V' is not on top of the racket handle but erring towards the bevel of the racket handle. You can mark the racket (as in the photo), so you can check your grip is correct at anytime.

Bevel

The bevel grip is used in many areas but its main use is for backhand overhead strokes. To get a bevel grip take a basic grip and simply move the thumb so it lies along the corner of the racket handle. This has the effect of moving the 'V' between the thumb and first finger slightly towards the top of the racket handle. Note the picture opposite shows the thumb fairly directly along the bevel – some players prefer it more diagonally across.

STROKE JARGON

When talking about badminton strokes, there are two phrases that you will often here:

- supination – this is rotating the forearm so that it is moving to a palm up position
- pronation – this is rotating the forearm so that it is moving to a palm down position

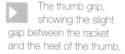
The basic grip, featuring the V-shape formed by the thumb and forefinger.

The bevel grip, showing the thumb along the corner of the racket handle.

Thumb

This grip is suitable for hitting shuttles on the backhand side that are well in front of the body. Holding the racket in the basic grip, turn in slightly to the right (for right handed players) or the left (for left handed players), so the thumb should form a slight diagonal across the back of the racket handle. There should be a gap between the heel of the thumb and the racket.

The thumb grip, showing the slight gap between the racket and the heel of the thumb.

THE SERVICE

There are basically two types of serve: the low and the high. The purpose of the low serve is to send the shuttle low over the net bringing the opponent forward creating space in the rear of the court and forcing a lift to stop the player attacking. The high serve is used when you want to move your opponent to the rear of the court.

THE LOW SERVE

The aim of the low serve is to send the shuttle from the front of your own service box into the front of the diagonally opposite service box, bringing your opponent forward thus creating space in the rearcourt and/or forcing a lift. You can play the serve either forehand or backhand.

Forehand Low Service

There are five key stages to the forehand low service.

1. Preparation

Adopt a balanced stance with your weight committed to the rear foot, close to the centre of the court. The shuttle is held out in front of your body with the racket back. A basic grip should to be used.

2. Release of the shuttle

Your weight starts to be transferred on to the front foot and the racket hip begins to move forward. The racket arm comes forwards with both a bent elbow and wrist. Eyes should be on the shuttle.

3. At impact

Impact is made to the side/in front of the body (45 degrees from the player). Push through the shuttle with a bent elbow and wrist (see picture opposite).

4. Follow through

Bring the racket up to threaten your opponent's reply.

Common faults

Beginners tend to make the following mistakes:

- hold the shuttle too far to the side
- take an excessive backswing
- use the wrist in the hitting action.

These mistakes lead to a loss of control and the shuttle travelling high above the net.

Backhand Low Service

There are four key stages to the backhand low service.

1. Preparation

Adopt a stance near the centre of the court with your feet side to side or one foot forward as preferred, with your weight balanced. Place the racket out in front of you, then place the shuttle onto the racket. The shuttle should be held well in front of the body below the waist, with a relaxed arm. A relaxed thumb-and-fingers grip should be used.

2. Backswing

Take the racket back, bending from the elbow, with a slight pronation of the arm. The non-racket arm should be kept still.

3. Forward swing and impact

The racket moves forward in the same arc as the backswing with the grip tightening on the racket. The non-racket hand should remain still. Release the shuttle at the last minute and hit the shuttle almost out of your hand.

4. Follow through

Follow through with a slight supination of the wrist and forearm, allowing the racket to move into a slightly elevated position. Let your eyes follow the shuttle to watch for your opponent's reaction.

Backhand low service: preparation.

Common faults

Beginners tend to hold both the racket and shuttle too close to their body. This stops them taking a long enough backswing. Many also fail to lift their elbow high enough. This means that their backswing does not begin from the elbow and results in them hitting using only a wrist action.

Forehand low service: impact.

THE BACKHAND FLICK SERVICE

There are four key stages to the backhand flick service.

1. Preparation

Adopt a stance near the centre of the court with your feet side to side or one foot forward as preferred, with your weight balanced. Place the racket out in front of you, then place the shuttle on to the racket. The shuttle should be held well in front of the body below the waist, with a relaxed arm. A relaxed thumb grip should be used.

2. Backswing

Take the racket back, bending from the elbow, with a slight pronation of the arm. The non-racket arm should be kept still.

3. Forward swing and impact

The racket moves forward **sharply** in the same arc as the backswing with the grip tightening on the racket. The non-racket hand should remain still. Release the shuttle at the last minute and hit the shuttle almost out of your hand.

4. Follow through

Continue to follow through with a slight supination of the wrist and forearm, allowing the racket to move into a slightly elevated position. Let your eyes follow the shuttle to watch for your opponent's reaction.

THE FOREHAND HIGH SERVE

The high serve is used mainly in singles. It is played from your own mid-court and the aim is to land the shuttle as deep as possible into the diagonally opposite service box, thereby creating space in the opponent's forecourt.

There are four key stages to the forehand high serve.

1. Preparation

Adopt a balanced stance with your weight committed to the rear foot close to the centre of the court. The shuttle is held out in front of your body with the racket back. A basic grip is to be used.

2. Release of the shuttle

The weight starts to be transferred on to the front foot and the racket hip begins to move forward. The shuttle is dropped and the racket is brought forward in an arc with the wrist hyperextended and the forearm supinating. Your eyes should be on the shuttle.

3. At impact

Impact is made in front of the body with contact below the waist. The wrist returns to a neutral position and the forearm starts to pronate. Your eyes should still be fixed on the shuttle. Your feet should remain in contact with the ground throughout the service.

4. Follow through

Your racket is at the limit of its forward travel, the forearm pronates as the relaxed follow through is completed. Your eyes follow the flight of the shuttle.

> **Groove your high serve by placing a racket in the back tramlines and trying to hit it. As you get better, aim to hit the target 10 times out of 10!**

Common faults

Beginners tend to swing across the shuttle rather than straight through and underneath it. This is often the result of holding the shuttle too close to or too far from the side of the body.

Many beginners also cut short their follow through and lean backwards. This does not allow the weight to move through to the front foot. As a result, the shuttle may fly high but usually well short of the back line.

Forehand high serve: release of the shuttle.

OVERHEAD STROKES

Forehand clear

The aim of the forehand clear is to hit the shuttle from your own rearcourt into the rearcourt of your opponent, moving him or her backwards to create space in the front of the court.

When the forehand clear is hit very high (a defensive clear), it creates time for you to recover to a position in the centre of the court. When the forehand clear is hit flatter (an attacking clear), it makes your opponent move quickly from the forecourt to the rearcourt.

There are four key stages to the forehand clear.

1. Preparation

The body should be positioned sideways to the net underneath the shuttle with a wide stance, knees bent and your weight on the back leg. Have a relaxed front arm with the hitting arm behind bent at the elbow. A basic grip should be adopted.

2. Before impact

Push off from your rear leg, commencing weight transfer to the front leg. As the hip starts to move forward the racket goes back behind the body. The eyes are focused on the shuttle and the racket arm supinates.

3. At impact

The shoulder and elbow of the racket arm follow the hip forward. The forearm starts to pronate as the arm reaches up towards the shuttle. The impact with the shuttle takes place almost directly above the hitting shoulder.

4. After impact

The racket follows through the intended direction of the shuttle. The forearm continues to pronate, and then moves across the body. The non-racket arm is brought in to control the body's rotation as the rear leg steps through to become the front foot.

Common faults

One common fault is when players do not get their body behind the shuttle. The player is then forced to strike the shuttle when it is actually behind them. Rather than transferring weight forwards into the stroke, their movement will be backwards after striking the shuttle. This will lead to a lack of power and direction.

Players hittting with too much wrist should use more forearm rotation.

 Forehand clear:
preparation.

 Forehand clear:
before impact.

Forehand clear:
after impact.

Forehand smash

The aim of the forehand smash is to hit a shuttle quickly from your own mid- or rearcourt into the midcourt of your opponent, bringing them forward to help create space in the rearcourt. The smash is the main attacking shot in badminton and is often hit to attempt to win a rally. It is played with almost the same technique as the forehand overhead clear but with one vital exception.

The point of impact should be forward of the shoulder which will cause the shuttle to travel downwards.

Common faults

Similar to the forehand overhead clear, players sometimes do not get behind the shuttle. Many newer players also tend to grip the racket too tightly throughout the whole shot, resulting in a restricted rotation/movement of the arm and therefore less power in the stroke. Remember to have a relaxed basic grip in preparation, which tightens as the racket head goes forwards.

 Forehand smash.

Forehand drop shot

The aim of the forehand drop shot is to hit a shuttle from your own rearcourt into the forecourt of your opponent, bringing them forward to help create space in the rearcourt. The preparation is the same as for the clear. Just before the racket hits the shuttle, the racket head's speed should be slower than that of a clear. This produces a slower shot which should fall just beyond the net.

Common faults

Some players tend to alter their hitting movement. Instead of taking a full swing and slowing the racket head's speed down, they 'pat' the shuttle gently. A patting action can be spotted by an opponent and will offer less control.

 Forehand drop shot.

Backhand clear

The aim of the backhand clear is to hit a shuttle when under pressure from your own deep backhand rearcourt into the rearcourt of your opponent, moving them backwards to create space in the front of the court. This will allow you time to recover your position.

There are three key stages to the backhand clear.

1. Preparation

The player turns so they have their back to the net. A bevel grip is adopted and the shuttle is approached with the racket head above the hand and a 90-degree angle is maintained between the forearm and racket. Lift the elbow and allow internal rotation of the upper arm whilst pronating the lower arm.

2. At impact

The arm starts to lift, but is not fully locked at the elbow. Supination of the forearm occurs and impact with the shuttle is made marginally behind and to the side of the body.

3. After impact

There is a small follow-through with a quick racket rebound.

Backhand clear: preparation.

Common faults

Many players don't keep their elbow down and racket head up in preparation for the shot. Players also use a full thumb grip, which means they cannot get the full face of their racket on to the shuttle. This will also restrict the ability of the upper/lower arm to rotate properly.

Note: establishing a 'point elbow in the air' position early in the shot preparation is another common fault which will limit the power.

 Backhand clear: impact.

 Backhand clear: after impact.

UNDERARM STROKES

Forehand net lift

The aim of the forehand net lift is to hit a shuttle from your own forecourt into the rearcourt of your opponent, sending them away from the base and allowing yourself time to recover.

There are three key stages to the forehand net lift.

1. Preparation

A basic grip should be adopted with a relaxed racket carriage. Begin to move the racket up in preparation for the hit. Start to lunge on to the racket leg towards the forecourt, forehand side. The forearm starts to supinate and the racket head moves outside the line of the shuttle.

2. At impact

The wrist is hyperextended as the hand is pushed forwards. Hit through the line of the shuttle.

3. After impact

The wrist returns to a neutral position while the forearm pronates.

Forehand net lift.

Backhand net lift

The aim of the backhand net lift is to hit a shuttle from your own forecourt into the rearcourt of your opponent, gaining time and making space in their forecourt.

There are three key stages to the backhand net lift.

1. Preparation

A thumb grip should be adopted with a relaxed racket carriage. Start the lunge towards the forecourt, backhand side, and draw the racket back in preparation for the shot while the forearm pronates. As you complete the lunge, your elbow begins to move upwards and forwards.

2. At impact

Extend the racket arm and supinate the forearm as you make contact with the shuttle.

3. After impact

Have a relaxed follow through and allow the arm to continue to supinate. The non-racket arm is extended back behind you to aid balance.

 Backhand net lift.

Forehand drive

The aim of the forehand drive is to hit a shuttle from your own mid- or rearcourt into the mid- or rearcourt of your opponent, moving your opponent away from their base and reducing their attacking options.

There are three key stages to the forehand drive.

1. Preparation

Adopt a relaxed basic grip with the racket moving towards the shuttle. Lunge out to the side with your forearm supinated and your upper arm externally rotated. The forearm supinates so much that momentarily the racket strings will be parallel with the ceiling.

2. At impact

Pronate the forearm towards the shuttle, creating an impact as early as possible.

3. After impact

The forearm continues to pronate through a shortened follow through as the racket is quickly stopped and moved back momentarily with a rebound action.

 Forehand drive:
just before impact.

Backhand drive

The aim of the backhand drive is to hit a shuttle from your own mid- or rearcourt into the mid- or rearcourt of your opponent, moving your opponent away from their base and reducing their attacking options.

There are three key stages to the backhand drive.

1. Preparation

Adopt a relaxed thumb grip with the racket moving towards the shuttle. Lunge out to the backhand side on your non-racket leg, or your racket leg if the shuttle is wider. Raise the elbow with the wrist hyperextended. Allow the upper arm to internally rotate and the lower arm to pronate so that the racket strings are parallel to the ceiling.

Backhand drive: preparation.

2. At impact

Externally rotate and supinate the lower arm while tightening the grip. Aim to create an impact with the shuttle in front of the body.

Common faults

One fault is to use a full thumb grip directly along the back of the racket handle, which restricts the rotation of the racket and the interaction of the thumb and fingers on the racket handle. Swinging with a flat racket face throughout the stroke, rather than making effective use of forearm rotation to help increase power, is another common fault.

Many players also do not turn their shoulders enough and do not use their non-racket arm effectively, thus reducing their balance and limiting their reach.

Forehand net shot

The aim of the forehand net shot is to hit a shuttle from your own forecourt into the forecourt of your opponent, bringing them forward to help create space in the rearcourt and to try to force a lift.

There are three key stages to the forehand net shot.

1. Preparation

Adopt a relaxed basic grip and racket carriage. Start to lunge towards the forehand forecourt and begin to raise the racket arm.

2. At impact

Present the racket strings towards the shuttle and drop the racket head below the hand. Tighten the grip slightly on impact and push the shuttle over the net using the forward momentum of your whole body.

3. After impact

The tighter your shot and the more under pressure your opponent is, the closer you stay to the net in order to kill a weak return.

Forehand net shot.

When playing a net shot don't play with a stiff arm and a tight grip, as this will cause the shuttle to travel too high and too far over the net. To get the net shot as tight as possible, use your fingers to manipulate the racket with a loose grip.

Backhand net shot

The aim of the backhand net shot is to hit a shuttle from your own forecourt into the forecourt of your opponent, bringing them forward to help create space in the rearcourt and to try to force a lift.

There are three key stages to the backhand net shot.

1. Preparation

Adopt a relaxed thumb grip and racket carriage. Start to lunge towards the backhand forecourt and begin to raise your racket arm.

2. At impact

Present the racket strings towards the shuttle and drop the racket head below the hand. Tighten the grip slightly on impact and push the shuttle over the net using the forward momentum of your whole body.

3. After impact

The tighter your shot and the more under pressure your opponent is, the closer you stay to the net in order to kill a weak return.

Backhand
net shot.

Receiving serve

Your stance is crucial when receiving service. You should have both knees flexed with your foot on the non-racket side of your body forward. Your racket should be positioned in front of your body at net height or slightly above. Try to stay alert and focused on your opponent's service action and the flight-path of the shuttle.

Reacting to a
short service.

Remember, you may have to react to a wide service, a short service or a high serve.

In singles and doubles receive serve standing in the centre of the service box. Since the service box for singles includes the back tramlines, this means you will receive serve slightly further back in singles. As you get better in doubles, you will learn to receive serve closer and closer to the front service line in order to threaten your opponent's low serve (see picture, left).

TACTICS

Tactics can be defined as:

- the strategy or plan devised prior to and implemented during a match
- the decisions made during and between rallies
- 'where, when and why we do something on court'.

DOUBLES FORMATIONS

Formations in doubles are essentially about both players establishing good base positions. The main two formations in doubles are established as a reaction to the position and height of the shuttle.

The attacking formation

If the shuttle is well above the height of the net with one player about to hit the shuttle then that team should be in, or moving to create, an attacking, front and back formation.

When using the attacking formation you should try to play shots that will allow you to keep the attack. These are mainly the drop shot and the smash from the rearcourt, net shots and kills from the forecourt.

The forecourt player should not be standing on the 'T' (they should be further back and slightly to the side that the shuttle is on). This will allow a greater chance for them to intercept the shuttle.

The defensive formation

If the opposing pair are about to hit the shuttle and it is well above the height of the net then you should be in or moving towards a side-by-side, defensive formation. This formation will give you the best chance of returning the opponents attacking shots.

When using the defensive formation you should try to play shots that the opposition cannot attack. These are

Always try to take the shuttle early as this gives your opponent less time and gives you more opportunity to attack. If you have to defend when playing doubles, then the more pressure you are under, the more you should consider lifting cross court. This gives you more time to recover and increases the chances of your partner being able to help out.

The team on the far side of the net are playing in the side-by-side defensive formation. The team on this side have adopted the back-and-front attacking system.

usually drives through the front opponent or net shots in front of your opponent. Your aim is to try to regain an attacking situation.

The defending players should not stand side by side on the court. The cross-court defender should stand slightly further forward than the defender on the straight, and both players should face the shuttle.

When attacking, your partner will expect a straight shot, so only play cross-court occasionally. Cross-court shots put your partner out of position and create large gaps on your side of the court for your opponents to exploit.

MIXED DOUBLES TACTICS

Mixed is essentially adapted level doubles. Generally, the aim should be to create situations where the man is in the rearcourt and the woman is at the net. Unfortunately, this has led to a very narrow definition of mixed doubles tactics, expressed simply as 'the women must go to the 'T' and stay there'. This is a very restrictive and ineffective view of mixed tactics.

Serving

When the man is serving, the woman takes up a position in the forecourt in front of the man. In this situation the woman is committing to covering the forecourt so the man must be aware of his responsibilities to cover the midcourt and rearcourt. The higher the level the further forwards the man tends to stand to serve.

Attacking

The ideal situation is with the man hitting down from the midcourt and rearcourt and the woman hitting down from the forecourt, with both players pressurising the opposing female player by channelling the attack on her (although at elite level, women's defences are so good that this tactic is changing).

Defending

When defending in mixed, as a general guideline, the woman tries to lift away cross-court as this allows her to take up a defensive

If your pair can control the net you have a big advantage in mixed doubles. Before and during the game, plan how you can control the net.

base slightly closer to the net. The man should lift straight to take any straight attacking replies. Using the width of the court on lifts effectively is vital to relieve pressure, particularly on the cross-court defender.

SINGLES

Success at singles relies on many things, including physical fitness, technical ability, psychological strength, etc. From a tactical perspective, the single court has more depth than width which means clears and drops are a good choice of shot. This is not to say that width can not be exploited, both width and height can be used, as well as depth, to out manoeuvre the opponent.

Finding a base

The term 'base' refers to the ideal court position reached that gives the best opportunity to cope with the opponent's probable replies. In singles there is no fixed position for the base.

ASSESSING YOUR OPPONENTS

In matches it is useful to assess your opponent to allow a tactical plan to be compiled. To do this you don't have to be a qualified coach, there are simple things you can look for to try to find your opponents' weaknesses.

Movement

Do they struggle to cover the whole court, are they slow to certain corners or do they have an insufficient fitness level to keep moving at the same pace for the whole match? If so it would be a good tactic to use the whole length and width of the court. One shot to the rearcourt followed by one shot to the forecourt would make your opponent cover the most ground and help exploit any weaknesses in their fitness or movement.

Size

Is your opponent a tall player? Most tall players will find it more difficult getting down to pick up shuttles low to the ground. They also struggle slightly to twist and turn quickly, so shots such as drops and smashes using the whole width of the court would be an ideal tactic against this type of player.

Shots

Most players have favourite shots that they play from certain corners. If you can work out what shots these are then it can help you to read the game and be quicker to shots. If a player, for example, mainly plays a cross-court drop from the rearcourt forehand then you can alter your body positioning to be more alert to move to the target corner. This may mean you are slower to the straight drop but you will be quicker to the cross-court drop, which will be the greater percentage of your opponent's shots.

> In order to win matches against better players than yourself you may have to alter the way you play in order to make the game as difficult as possible for your opponent to win.

England's Gail Emms is known for her tactical awareness and ability to read her opponents.

PRE-GAME PREPARATION

When played competitively, badminton is a fast, action-packed game. It places a lot of stresses and strains on your body as you have to twist, turn and stretch to reach the shuttle. This is why it is important to make sure that your body is properly prepared before you start any game or practice session.

PREPARE TO PLAY

Active muscles produce heat and work more efficiently than cold muscles. Preparing to play involves 'activity' to get the muscles warmer so that you will play better and reduce the likelihood of injuring yourself by, for example, pulling a muscle.

The smaller the muscle mass, the quicker the muscles will warm up. As a result, adults must do a longer warm up than children.

There are a number of stages to the warm-up phase:

Activity

Use simple activities that involve raising the heart rate and muscle temperature, such as jogging, for 2–5 minutes in order to improve muscle elasticity, raise heart rate and increase blood flow.

Stretch

A game of badminton will involve all major muscle groups so it is important to have a thorough stretch. Our muscles are already warm so usually we don't want to do any static stretches allowing our muscles to become cold. Use dynamic stretching (increasing muscle elasticity prior to exercise via the use of controlled mobility exercises), such as lunges and squats. Please note, if you have been advised to do static stretches or feel it is necessary to static stretch then you should do so.

Stability

Stability is an important component of preparing to play because it activates the balance sensors and stabilising muscle groups.

PHYSIO/DOCTOR ADVICE

Before participating in any badminton related or physical activity you should consult a doctor, physiotherapist or other suitably qualified practitioner.

This reduces the possibility of injuries. There are a number of areas that you should focus on, such as:

- ankle
- abdominals
- back
- gluteals
- shoulder.

Speed

Speed is a major component of badminton, fast adjustments of the feet, forwards, backwards and laterally are very important. Exercises such as fast feet, short sprints and running backwards with short sharp steps should be completed in 3–5 second bursts with 15–25 seconds recovery.

Shadow

Shadowing movements on court in order to link a number of movements and incorporate rapid changes of direction and will get the body adjusted to the type of movement you are about to perform.

Knock-up

Before you start it is highly recommended to go through a range of shots on court. This involves playing shots from clears right through to net shots in order to get used to the speed of the shuttle and the playing environment. Remember to practice both forehand and backhand shots.

> **In doubles, players knock up with their playing partner. In singles, players knock up with their opponent.**

Nathan Robertson and Gail Emms knocking up.

BADMINTON IN SCHOOLS AND CLUBS

BADMINTON England's educational programmes and resources provide support from Key Stage 1 through to GCSE and A level. The BIG (Badminton Is Great) programme, and the Badminton Into Schools Initiative (Bisi) cater for classroom and club delivery. The programmes and activities focus on establishing the foundations of movement literacy, refining and reinforcing these throughout a child's motor development, alongside the teaching and coaching of badminton racket and games skills.

THE BIG PROGRAMME

Divided into five phases, the programme starts with the principles of primary patterns of movement through to learning how to improve, train and compete. The series' comprehensive and unique introduction underpins all motor development and provides the foundation for all badminton activity, as well as benefiting young players as all-round athletes. It is suitable for both teachers and coaches and is ideal to be used in both educational lessons and club sessions.

BIG Phase 1 (3–7 year olds)

This stage establishes the BIG pathway with the seven primary movement patterns (gait, squat, lunge, bend/flexion, push, pull and rotate/twist) through fun activities.

BIG Phase 2 (5–8 year olds)

The pathway continues through the primary patterns and focuses on the six components of function (planes of movement, momentum control, postural stability, dynamic flexibility, loading and unloading and dynamic balance). Again, this is delivered through fun activities.

BIG Phase 3a and 3b (9–14 year olds)

Phase 3a covers agility, balance, coordination, speed (ABCS) and strength (continuing with the development of movement and athleticism), while phase 3b introduces technical and badminton-specific foundation criteria.

To find out more about Bisi and BIG, contact the development department at BADMINTON England.

Games, Activities and Ideas Cards

The Bisi 'Games, Activities and Ideas' cards are designed to provide badminton teachers and coaches (levels 1 and 2) with extra ideas and activities to enhance the BIG programme:

- Key stage 1: 5–9 year olds
- Key stage 2: 7–11 year olds
- Key stage 2/3: 9–14 year olds.

BIG Junior Awards Scheme

The awards scheme supports junior development throughout each phase of the BIG programme, and is linked to all the resources.

WHAT DO SCHOOLS GET?

By affiliating to BADMINTON England, schools will receive:

- quarterly information on new developments
- magazine
- information about local, regional and national tournaments and competitions
- opportunities to attend top class badminton events
- reduced cost resources, training and updates.

Affiliated schools also have the opportunity to apply for Badminton Academy School Status.

BIG Phase 4a and 4b (13+ years old)

Phase 4a focuses on getting stronger, fitter and faster. This supports the content of phase 4b which considers the development of technical and tactical ability.

BIG Phase 5 (14+ years old)

The final phase enables students to learn how to improve, train and compete in the game of badminton. It covers both technical and tactical skills to a high level, aspects of fitness, training and athletic movement.

RESOURCES AND EQUIPMENT

Rackets

The Bisi equipment range offers six different sizes and standard of racket, exclusive to BADMINTON England. These range from the Bisi Mini used by juniors to the Bisi Graphite for the older and more skilful player.

FURTHER INFORMATION

BADMINTON FOR THE DISABLED

Badminton has become a popular game among people with disabilities and there are a number of special coaching courses available. In response to this increase in popularity, the rules of the game have been amended to account for a variety of disabilities. Amendments include the post and net height and service action and faults.

Rules for versions of the game involving sitting players, players in wheelchairs and standing players are found in the appendices of the Laws of Badminton.

ADMINISTRATION OF THE GAME

Badminton is administered worldwide by the International Badminton Federation (IBF). It has over 150 full-time member nations, which makes it one of the largest sporting bodies in the world. It is responsible for the management of the world team championships for men and women who compete for the Thomas Cup and the Uber Cup respectively. It also helps with development, approves equipment and assesses and accredits officials.

The IBF's website can be found at: www.internationalbadminton.org. The website contains the full Laws of Badminton and its appendices, which are downloadable and viewable in PDF format.

Badminton is a sport for all. There are different rules and courses available to support people with disabilities who are keen to get involved.

BADMINTON ENGLAND

BADMINTON England is the sport's governing body in England. It actively promotes and encourages the sport's development at every level – from grass roots through clubs, local leagues and county organisations to the National Squad.

Many categories of membership are available including supporters, club and county up to the World Class squad. BADMINTON England offers information about the game and coaching courses, runs tournaments from county to international level and sells books and videos. For further information contact:

BADMINTON England
National Badminton Centre
Milton Keynes MK8 9LA

Tel: 01908 268400
Fax: 01908 268412

E-mail:
enquiries@badmintonengland.co.uk

Website:
www.badmintonengland.co.uk

THE NATIONAL BADMINTON MUSEUM

The National Badminton Museum was launched in 2003. It is run by volunteers and has no guaranteed income. Limited office accommodation, storage area and display areas are provided by BADMINTON England in the National Badminton Centre.

The museum, which is unmanned, can be visited whenever the National Badminton Centre is open, and consists of a small area devoted to the history of badminton, several display cabinets in various locations, a poster collection in the restaurant and a collection of badminton-related prints in the bar and quiet area.

In addition the museum houses past badminton magazines, a collection of badminton books, minute books of the Association, documents and so on. These can be viewed by appointment. If you have any queries please contact:
Museum@badmintonengland.co.uk

BADMINTON
ENGLAND

Play it. Love it. Live it.

BADMINTON CHRONOLOGY

1893 The Badminton Association formed in Southsea, Hampshire on 13 September by 14 clubs.

1899 First Badminton Association Championships played.

1901 Rectangular courts replaced the hourglass-shaped courts at the All England Championships.

1903 First international badminton match played. England beat Ireland in Dublin 5–2.

1907 Scoring in Ladies' Singles changed. Played to 11 instead of 15.

1907 The final of the men's doubles at the All England Championships was postponed owing to failing light and completed four days later.

1908 First international tournament outside England played in Dieppe, France.

1909 Straight feathers in shuttlecocks adopted for All England, in place of barrel-shaped shuttlecocks.

1914 Guy Sautter won the singles at the All England using a pseudonym Un Lapin, so that his employers did not know where he was!

1928 Sir George Thomas won the men's doubles at the All England, his twenty-first title, a total that has never been passed.

1930 Inter-County Championships competition launched. Middlesex were the first winners, beating Northumberland 13–2.

1933 Two sisters from England reached the final of the All England singles, Leoni Kingsbury beating Thelma Kingsbury.

1934 The International Badminton Federation formed with 9 founder members. The Badminton Association became the Badminton Association of England.

1947 A blizzard on the eve of the All England caused snow to be driven horizontally into the hall. Six matches instead of sixty played on first day.

1948–49 First competition for the Thomas Cup. An international championship for men – the cup presented by Sir George Thomas, was won by Malaya.

1951 The BBC televised part of the All England play – on Friday both mixed semi-finals and on Saturday most of the play was screened.

1954 First World Invitation Tournament played in Glasgow.

1956–57 Uber Cup launched. An international team competition for ladies on the lines of the Thomas Cup. The trophy presented by Mrs Betty Uber and won on the first occasion by the USA.

1960 Heather Guntrip (Kent, England) was drawn against the number one seed in all three events at the All England.

1964 In the final of the ladies' doubles of the All England Ulla Rasmussen and her sister Karin Jorgensen (Denmark) beat sisters Judy Hashman and Sue Peard (USA).

1965 The English Schools Badminton Association founded at a meeting in Manchester. It was dissolved in 2000 to become part of the Badminton Association of England Ltd.

1966 Badminton included in the eighth Commonwealth Games for the first time. The Games were held in Kingston, Jamaica.

1967 European Badminton Union formed.

1977 First sponsored All England. John Player provided financial assistance until 1982.

1977 First World Championships played in Malmo, Sweden.

1979 First Open Tournament – Masters Event at the Royal Albert Hall. Sponsored by Friends Provident Life Office. Total prize money £21,000.

1980 In July the Badminton Association of England moved offices from Bromley in Kent to a farmhouse at Loughton Lodge, Milton Keynes. On this site the magnificent National Badminton Centre has since been developed.

1983 Yonex sponsored the All England for the first time. They are still sponsoring the event after 23 years and their present contract continues until the end of the 2009 event.

1992 Badminton included as a competitive sport for the first time in the Olympic Games held in Barcelona.

1994 Yonex All England Championships moved to Birmingham.

2000 Simon Archer and Jo Goode (England) won bronze medals at the Olympic Games in Sydney.

2004 Nathan Robertson and Gail Emms of England won silver medals at the Olympic Games held in Athens.

2005 The Badminton Association of England Ltd. renamed BADMINTON England.

GLOSSARY

Backhand
A stroke hit on the left of the body by right-handed players, and on the right of the body by left-handers.

Base
The ideal court position, giving the best opportunity to cope with the opponent's probable replies.

Chassé
Punchy steps, both long and short, where there is no crossing of the feet, nor do the feet come together. One foot is often at 90 degrees to the direction of travel, and hips are also often at 90 degrees to the direction of travel.

Clear
A powerful overhead shot played from the rearcourt to the opponent's rearcourt with a relatively high trajectory.

Cross behind
Non-racket leg crossing behind the racket leg, foot usually at 90 degrees to the direction of travel.

Cross-court
A stroke played diagonally across the court.

Drive
A fast, flat stroke played to the mid- or rearcourt of the opponent.

Drop shot
A relatively soft overhead shot played from the rearcourt to the opponent's forecourt.

Feeding
Placing the shuttle correctly in the air to maximise the efficiency of practice.

Forecourt
The front third of the court.

Forehand
A stroke hit on the right of the body by right-handed players, and on the left of the body by left-handers

Game point
The score when a player needs only one more point to win the game.

Hyperextension (wrist)
The wrist being bent back so the back of the hand is moved as close as possible to the back of the forearm (making an angle of about 90 degrees).

Kick-through
A movement forming part of the hitting action, often taking place in the rearcourt. It involves the racket foot being driven actively off the ground so it moves forwards and changes from being the back foot to the front foot.

Let
A call for a particular point to be replayed when interrupted for whatever reason. Alternatively, in a match without an umpire, used when the players can't agree on a line call.

Lift
An underarm shot that is played from the forecourt to the opponent's rearcourt with an initial upward trajectory.

Love
Denotes zero points.

Lunge

A large step by either leg, with the lead foot landing in the direction of travel and front knee bending in alignment with the landing foot.

Match point

The score when a player needs only one more point to win the match.

Mid-court

The middle third of the court.

Net shot

A shot played from the forecourt to the forecourt of your opponent.

Overhead

Describes a stroke played above the head – a clear, for example.

Pronation

Rotation of the forearm so that it is moving to a palm-down position. This is a main characteristic of the forward swing on forehand shots.

Rally point scoring

The new scoring system, in which the winner is the first player to score 21 points. A point is awarded to the winner of each rally.

Rearcourt

The rear third of the court.

Running steps

Steps taken with the feet, hips and head all pointing in the same direction of travel.

Shadowing

Mimicking badminton movements without hitting a shuttle.

Split-drop

Used as a starting step in response to an opponent's hit. It involves widening the stance and bending the knees.

Stroke-cycle

The name given to a complete stroke, including the components 'start', 'approach', 'hitting action' and 'recovery'. It is very useful in fault correction.

Supination

Rotation of the forearm so that it is moving to a palm-up position. This is often done when taking the racket back in preparation for forehand shots.

Tactics

The strategy or plan devised prior to and implemented during a match; the decisions made during and between rallies; and the 'where, when and why we do something on court'.

Technique

How we do something on court.

Traditional scoring

The conventional method of scoring, in which the winner is the first to 15 points (11 in ladies' singles), and where points can only be scored on the serve.

Tramlines

The area at the sides of the doubles court which is not used in singles play.

Umpire

The umpire decides which player has won a point and also keeps the score. In major tournaments the umpire is assisted by line judges.

Unforced error

An error made while under no pressure from the opponent.

QUESTIONS & ANSWERS

Now that you have read the rules and played a few games, try tackling these questions to see how well you know the ins and outs of Badminton. The answers are on the next page.

Questions

1. The area within which the server must stand is clearly defined. Must the server's partner stand within the opposite service area?

2. Is it okay for a server or receiver to have their foot on one or more lines which mark the service court?

3. Must the shuttle be over the area defined as the correct service court at the moment it is hit?

4. What happens when a service that touches the top of the net and is obviously going to be a fault is touched by the receiver's clothing before it hits the floor?

5. In a doubles match the side which wins one game must commence serving in the next game. Which partner has to do this?

6. If, when serving, you completely miss contacting the shuttle, is this a fault?

7. How long must the receiver stay in the diagonally opposite half court to the server?

8. Are there any limitations on the position of the receiver's partner?

9. Once the service is delivered, what limitations are there on the positions of the players in a doubles?

10. If, in a doubles game, one of the players starts in the right half-court, they stay there whenever their side's score is even. If, later on during the game, it is discovered that they are in the wrong half-court, should the player and partner immediately change sides?

11. If you are not ready to receive a serve but nevertheless make an attempt to return it, can you claim a 'let' because you were not ready?

12. What is the decision if the shuttle touches the roof in play?

13. What is the decision if the shuttle is deflected by a girder overhead?

14. What happens if a shuttle, after passing over the net, gets caught by its feathers on the net tape or mesh and remains there?

15. If a player hits the shuttle with one contact only but that contact is the racket frame, is that a fair shot?

16. If a shuttle is only just falling over the net or may drop onto the net tape, can you lean over the net with your racket?

17. If a player hits a wide shuttle round the post clearly below the level of the top of the net, but it falls on the line, is this a fair shot or not?

18. When there is no umpire, should a player call their own faults, or should they wait for the opponents to claim them?

19. Can a player call to their partner to take a shuttle or leave it because it may be going out of court?

Answers

1. No. The player may stand where they like provided that they do not unsight the receiver. The receiver is entitled to a clear and uninterrupted view of the shuttle (Law 9.7).

2. No. A foot on the line is held to be outside the service court and is therefore a fault (Laws 9.1.2 and 9.2).

3. No. The restrictions from where the service shall be delivered are imposed only on the player's feet. Players can lean or extend their racket beyond the lines (Law 9).

4. A fault against the receiver and the server wins the point (Law 13.2.5).

5. Either partner may serve, but must do so from the right-hand court (Laws 11.9 and 11.5).

6. Yes (Law 9.3).

7. Some part of both of the receiver's feet must remain in contact with the court in a stationary position from the start of the service (Law 9.4), until the shuttle is actually struck by the server. Then the receiver can step out.

8. There are no restrictions at all provided that the player does not unsight the server in any way (Law 9.7).

9. There are only two limitations. Firstly, the player must not prevent an opponent from making a legal stroke where the shuttle is followed over the net (Law 13.4.4). Secondly, they must not invade the opponents' court with racket or person so that an opponent is obstructed or distracted (Laws 13.4.2 and 13.4.3).

10. No. If the mistake is not discovered at once, they should remain where they are and continue play (Law 12.2).

11. No. A player is deemed to be ready if an attempt is made to return the shuttle (Law 9.5).

12. It is a fault (Law 13.2.4). In special circumstances, however, it may be a 'let' under local by-laws.

13. You should enquire about this prior to play. Law 13.2.6 gives the local badminton authority power to make a by-law concerning such a matter.

14. It counts as a 'let' except during service (Law 14.1.3).

15. Yes. It is a fair shot. The law was altered in 1963.

16. No. That would be an invasion of your opponents' court. You must wait until the shuttle has passed over the net. In making your stroke you may follow through with your racket over the net provided that at the moment of contact the shuttle is on your side (Law 13.3).

17. It is a fair shot.

18. You should always call your own faults and should call them immediately. When a game is played with an umpire, it is the umpire's duty to call them.

19. Yes. The two players form a team, and they may assist each other how they like. But no spectator should ever give advice during play.

INDEX